Abhirami Edoor Manoj

Abhirami Edoor Manoj 14-year-old student in 10th grade at Sharjah Indian School, I have always been fascinated by the power of words and the ability they have to shape our thoughts, dreams, and perspectives. Growing up in a family that values education and creativity guided by my loving parents, Manoj Edoor Krishnan kutty (MD , Manoj And Associates Chartered Accountants) and Shyma Manoj (Civil Engineer) Sister, Anagha Edoor Manoj
Mob: 0526309975

English Language
Lamps of Love
(Poems)
by
Abhirami Edoor Manoj

◆

Published in October 2021
by Kairali Books Private Limited
Thalikkavu Road, Kannur.
Ph : 0497-2761200
E-Mail : kairalibooksknr@gmail.com

◆

Cover Design
Prasanth Mangad

◆

88/24-25/Sl.No.1655/200/NS.18.6

Lamps of Love

Abhirami Edoor Manoj

Kairali Books

Coents

Preface

At this young age, I am driven by a desire to share my thoughts with others and contribute in some small way to the world around me. This book is a reflection of my observations, imagination, and the lessons I've learned along the way. As I continue my education and personal growth, I hope this endeavor will encourage other young people to follow their passions and embrace the limitless potential of learning and creativity.

I would like express my gratitude to my parents, my sister, teachers and friends who inspired me during the writing of this book.

I look forward to the future with excitement, and I hope you enjoy reading this book as much as I enjoyed writing it.

Sincerely,
Abhirami Edoor Manoj

Pearl Beads

All the beads
I had fell to the ground,
scattered and shattered.
Those beads flew away somewhere,
and I couldn't gather them up.
It was only when they were lost that I realized
how dear they were to me.
I understood the pain of a loss that would
never be recovered.

To Stand as a Petal

Even though I knew
I would be startled,
I did not wish
To be trampled upon
Like a fallen dry leaf.
I only hoped
To stand as a petal,
Gently swaying
Forever with the soft breeze.
That's all I ever wanted.

"Endless Showers"

In every passing shower,
My eyes brimmed with tears.
No matter how much it rained,
My thirst remained unquenched.
Again and again,
I longed for the skies to weep,
But those dark clouds
Loomed without breaking.
Within my heart,
Even after all that rain,
The showers never ceased.
Those drops of life,
Kept falling again and again,
As tears from my eyes.

Twilight's Enchantment

In the lightning of the Thula month,

During the twilight hour,

As you glow and shimmer,

Oh evening, how beautiful you are!

Each flash of lightning,

Scattering silver light,

Falls upon you,

And it feels as though

You are bathed in shades of saffron.

How many colors has nature

Bestowed upon you,

Oh evening!

You are such an enchanting beauty,

That your boundless charm

Fills me with envy.

Love That Merged and Dissolved

What is love?

I did not know.

To understand it,

I loved nature,

And I discovered what love is.

I loved the beautiful flowers,

And I learned the fragrance of love.

I loved the butterflies

That sipped nectar from the flowers,

And I understood the sweetness of love.

I loved the rain,

And I felt the coolness of love.

In that experience of love,

I merged and dissolved.

Love transforms the lover,

Leaving her delicate and fragile.

Dreams Bound and Tied

The tinkling glass bangles
Adorn my wrists,
But I long to walk freely.
The jingling anklets
Echo as I move,
But I wish to dance and play.
To hold the white doves in my hands
And let them fly with me,
There are countless unfulfilled desires
That linger within me.

Lamps of Love

Do you know, my Lord,
That you are the rhythm of my heartbeat?
The lamps of love,
Which I have carefully guarded within my
heart,
I have encircled them with the chambers of my
heart,
Not allowing them to extinguish.
I fear, my Lord,
That if those lamps somehow go out,
The light of the ones I rekindle
May not shine as brightly.

Solitary Showers

I am a rain cloud,
Eager to pour down.
Though I long
To release my rains,
I never wish
To rain before others.
Even when I yearn
To pour and weep inside,
What I truly desire
Is to rain and cease,
Alone, in solitude.

Little Dreams

The little dreams

That once slept within my heart

Have turned into an unquenchable thirst.

The place they once stayed
Has slipped away,
And I was somehow too weak to let them soar.
My dreams wandered off
To some unknown place,
And none of them ever returned.
The dreams knew well
The heat within me,
That I would pluck them away
Like a tender leaf.

Flickers of Desire

Like the fireflies
Dancing and flickering
In the blue sky,
Like the floating tufts
Of dandelion seeds,
Like the petals
Swaying gently in the breeze,
My heart yearns deeply
To shine just once,
To soar and glide,
To dance and play.

Love Like a Bubble

What is the meaning of love?
What is purity?
Is love something
To be begged for or given?
Never.
Love is something
To be mutually understood,
Given and received.
Otherwise,
Love becomes nothing more
Than a fragile bubble,
Ready to burst
At any moment.

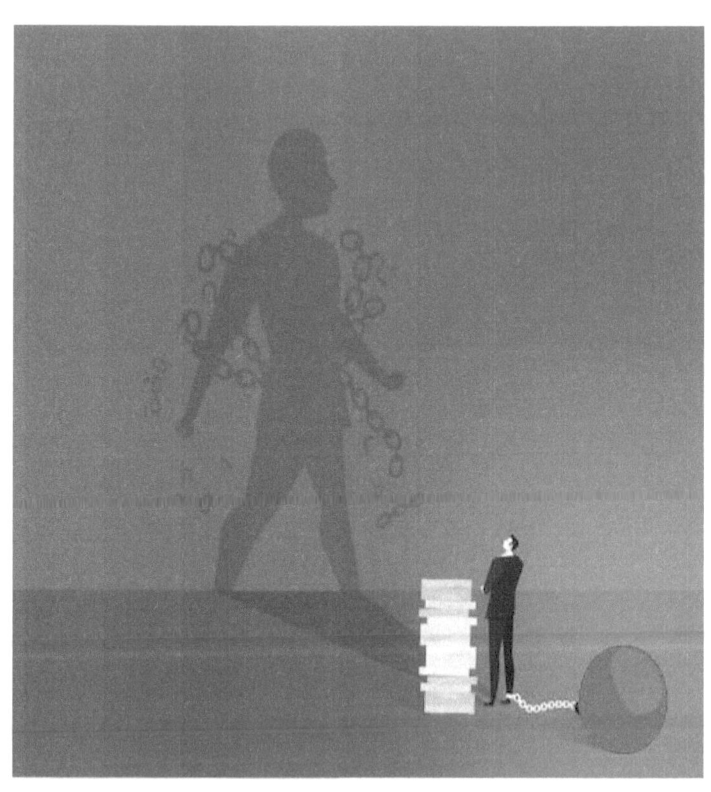

The Ultimate Truth

Could I create a heaven
Here on earth?
I was doubtful,
Asking myself repeatedly.
My mistaken belief
Was that it couldn't be done.
I spoke with nature,
And nature whispered to me:
"You can create heaven within yourself.
Love yourself,
Talk to yourself,
Know yourself.
Open your heart and smile.
You can create heaven within,
And experience the bliss of it."
Wasn't nature's whisper the truth?
Yes, the truth—
The ultimate truth.

Flowers of Sorrow

Pain blossoms
In the corners of my eyes,
As I search endlessly
For just a little love.
In my tear-filled eyes,
Where flowers of sorrow
Always bloom,
I had wished
For love to overflow instead.

Under the Sharoan Tree

Under the Sharoan tree,
Flowers blossomed,
The fragrances
Were like divine blooms,
In that Sharoan tree,
I witnessed
The colors spilling
In the twilight,
I flew like a Sharik bird,
Never wishing to return,
In that Sharoan tree,
I transformed
Into a dweller of the moment.

Dear Friend

Like flowers blooming in the sky,
What a joy it is to see you,
Oh dear friend,
When I behold your beauty,
My inner flower rejoices.
Like scattered petals
Falling like drizzling rain,
With the charm of your movements,
If for just a moment,
You do not come close to me,
I feel the heat of longing,
Oh dear friend.

The Messenger of Dreams

Through the cool dreams of the hills,
My heart wandered,
Through the open window,
To add grace to my dreams,
The quil flew
To my side.
Are you also soaring
Through the cool dreams of the hills?

In the Embrace of Rain

Wrapped in fog,
The cool rain fell,
To erase the chill,
I unknowingly found you,
Who is this co-dweller,
Merged within me?
To share with you,
Forever in the cool rain,
I long to bathe.

Fleeting Aspirations

After the fresh rain,
The earth had the scent of new soil,
When dreams walk,
The longing was immense
For them to grow and blossom.
From the rain-soaked new soil,
The dreams I planted
Quickly sprouted and emerged
When the sun's heat fell upon them,
Just as swiftly,
All my dreams,
Suddenly withered away.
Never again
Were there dreams within me
To nurture and cultivate.

In the Realm of Shadows
Darkness

I was in slumber,
The sun, the moon,
And the stars
Visited one after another,
Unaware, I remained in sleep.
In which world
Had I arrived?
There were no sun, moon, or stars;
There was no warmth,
No chill;
In that realm of darkness,
I was the only one,
Claiming that world
As my own.

At banks of River Chitra

In a charming space,
An artist painted
A beauty, like a full moon,
A painting that was priceless,
And it was given a name.
Those who came, enchanted
By the allure of the painting,
Left in disappointment,
For that beautiful image
Belonged only to the artist.